The Online Passive Income Business Guide for Beginners:

How to Earn Monthly Income on Autopilot and Gain Financial Freedom for Life

James Umber

I0484190

James Umber

ISBN-13: 978-1508945475

ISBN-10: 1508945470

CONTENTS

1. INTRODUCTION — PG. 6
2. WHAT IS PASSIVE INCOME? — PG. 9
3. WHO CAN EARN PASSIVE INCOME? — PG. 12
4. THE BENEFITS OF PASSIVE INCOME — PG. 15
5. HOW TO EARN PASSIVE INCOME — PG. 19
6. CHOOSING NICHES AND ADVERTISING — PG. 22
7. INCOME FROM E-BOOKS — PG. 26
8. INCOME FROM YOUTUBE — PG. 32
9. AFFILIATE MARKETING — PG. 36
10. THE DANGERS OF PASSIVE INCOME — PG. 42
11. FINAL THOUGHTS — PG. 25

1. INTRODUCTION

In the past, there was no real alternative to working a 9 to 5 job unless you were rich already and could hire other people to do your work for you.

So most people just accepted that this is the way things were and worked their entire lives, earning their boss money in return for a mediocre wage. A lot of people are still doing this now.

Is this how you want to live your life? Or do you want to gain financial freedom with hardly any initial investment? Because it's possible, now more than ever. All it requires is some hard work and determination.

Thanks to the internet we have access to countless ways of earning money online. Yes there are a lot of scams out there like survey websites that promise you money and never pay you. But who wants to sit there filling those things out anyway? What I'm proposing in this book is not only a thousand times easier but it can also earn you thousands. And I'm not talking thousands a year I'm talking thousands a month.

Thousands a year via passive income is actually pretty easy in all honesty if you know how to do it. It's the same as everything in life, take web design for example. I can design a website in about 2 hours that I charge about £700 for. But that's because I know how to do it and most people don't.

So, with the information you're about to learn, you will be able to do what most people can't. We will forget about years and we will be aiming for something more like 2 thousand a month and then build from there.

James Umber

2. WHAT IS PASSIVE INCOME?

There are two main types of business, service based and product based. Service based businesses provide a service which they carry out for their clients in return for money. Product based businesses work by selling their customers products in exchange for money.

Now traditionally both of these types of business require you to either carry out the service on offer or to provide the product to the customer. This obviously requires effort. In an ideal world, we would be doing something else with our time and saving our effort for things we actually want to do rather than working away in exchange for money.

By setting up a passive income business, we only do the work once to get things up and running and then it just ticks away in the background earning us money from that point onwards. Imagine if all jobs were like that! If a builder could just build one house and then get paid for it every month. They would be jumping for joy.

But think about it, they could build the house and rent it out. If they build a few more they can live off the money and never have to build another house again. That's what passive income is, and it's entirely possible.

Now obviously passive income doesn't mean you can literally do nothing and suddenly magic money will appear out of nowhere and float into your pocket. You do have to set up work, but as I said you only do it once.

So don't think that it's an easy ride as the set up work will take a lot of time and effort and some trial and error to get perfect. But once you have got your process down you will be able to set up multiple passive income streams that will truly earn you money on autopilot.

3. WHO CAN EARN PASSIVE INCOME?

This one is easy. Anyone can earn passive income. From teenagers to the older generation. From stay at home parents to full time workers. As long as you have a computer and an internet connection then the world is your oyster!

The thing it does take, that some people just don't have, is motivation and dedication. You need to have the motivation to really get this new passive income business up and running and the dedication to keep at it if it doesn't work right away.

If you work full time, for the best and quickest results, you will need to be able to have the will power to get in from a day's work and work on your new business. Then on weekends, work more. It does take work to get things moving, but once it's done, you will look back and be so glad you did it.

If you're a student, you may have to sacrifice a little bit of your social life in order to get this working for you properly as it does take time to get things going. This is because you don't want to sacrifice your studies so you will need to give up some more free time. I might actually have a few tips later on in the book on how you guys can use your college or university work to actually earn you money so stay tuned for that!

For those of you who don't work or if you're a stay at home

parent for example, you will have to be able to manage your time around your day to day tasks to give you enough time to work on your business. You are also less likely to have any personal money to invest in your business but that's fine, it can pretty much all be set up for free anyway.

The younger ones among you will probably be good with computers but you may also get distracted easier. I'm not too old myself and I can tell you that, although I'm way past being a teenager now, a lot of my friends still prefer to go out drinking and play video games rather than work on bettering their lives.

So while I'm sitting here writing this book they are probably on the PlayStation. If you're going to do that and not work on building your business then you will not succeed.

Those of you who are older and less tech savvy are going to have it the hardest. If you're completely computer illiterate then I would definitely suggest going on some kind of crash course to learn how to use a computer as it will make your life much easier in the long run when starting your business.

Overall though I'm going to try and keep things as simple as I can so that anyone can do it.

James Umber

4. THE BENEFITS OF PASSIVE INCOME

When you're just starting out and you have things up and running, you might be earning a hundred or two hundred pounds a month passive income. The benefits will start to show even at this point.

You will just check your account one day and you will think, I didn't know I had that much money. Then you will remember, your passive income payment has come in. This is a great feeling, and it happened to me a few times when I was starting out. I would just forget it was coming in and then be really excited when I checked my balance.

Even this small amount of extra money every single month will enable you to do many things and it will mean something different for everyone.

Maybe it will enable to finally start paying off some of that debt that's hanging over your head. Maybe it will take the pressure off and enable you to have a bit more fun and be less stressed. Or maybe it will mean you can start putting some savings away for a rainy day.

Then after some more work on your business you will be able to scale this up and maybe start earning a thousand a month.

This is when things start to really get interesting. This will enable you to live just as you were before but now your money worries are gone. You have your wage coming in plus another thousand on top!

With this you can quickly start to get rid of debt, turn down overtime, save money quickly or even save for a few months and get yourself a new car or take your family on a dream holiday.

Then we get to the 2 thousand pounds a month milestone. This is where most people would probably consider leaving their job, unless you're one of the lucky individuals who actually likes our job!

Even if you do like your job, you could maybe do less hours. For those of you who quit, this has the obvious benefit of giving you the gift of time. Time to do what you want, when you want. And the best bit is, during the time that you're doing whatever it is you feel like doing that day, your passive income business is still ticking away behind the scenes earning you money!

The main benefit of passive income in my opinion however is the scalability. For example if you're earning 100 pounds a day, there is no reason at all why you can't just set up something pretty much exactly the same again and double your income to 200.

Once you have earned your first 100 in a month. You will know how you did it, so you can just do it again. But this time it will be easier and faster.

From there, the sky is the limit. Also, when you start earning a lot, you can actually start to outsource some of the set up work by hiring a virtual assistant or someone to make your informational products or set up your promotional sites for you for example. This will mean that the only hard part about passive income, the set up process, is now being partially done for you too!

James Umber

5. HOW TO EARN PASSIVE INCOME

In order to earn passive income online you will need assets. Assets are usually made to either sell as a digital download or to generate traffic in order to display adverts or affiliate links.

My favorite way to earn passive income is via digital downloads of informational products. I do this in the form of e-books. With informational products like e-books you can simply list it online and then it will just sell multiple times with each buyer getting a downloadable copy.

Once you have a book online, your work is done and it will generate you income on autopilot. That is unless you want to do some extra marketing work over time which is up to you. This is the same with things like stock photos, video courses, stock vectors, etc. All of these things can be classed as an asset.

As I mentioned there is also the option of using an asset such as a website or a video to draw traffic in. Once you have the traffic there, you can have adverts and affiliate links displaying on your content.

Each time an advert is clicked, you get a percentage of the money the advertiser is paying to show that advert. Affiliate links however work slightly differently in that you essentially refer your traffic to another site where they have to make a purchase. When they buy something, the site that you referred them to pays you for sending the customer to them. All of this is also on autopilot.

I will go into more detail on how each of these things work over the next few chapters. But to recap, you need to create online assets and then monetize them somehow by either charging for them, showing adverts on them or via referrals.

Obviously, it's all well and good having these assets out there, but what good are they if they just get lost in the endless abyss of the internet? We need as many people as possible to find them, luckily there are a lot of ways to make this quite easy. But first we need a niche...

⁇

6. CHOOSING NICHES AND ADVERTISING

The first thing to consider when advertising your asset is choosing the subject matter and what niche you will be in. You should think about the niche and the keywords before you even create your asset.

I realize I'm throwing a lot of words about here and this is a beginners guide to lets break it down a bit.

So we know that an asset is our product or content that is generating us either sales, advert clicks or referrals to our affiliates.

Our niche is the specific market that our asset is aimed at. I can't stress the importance of choosing a good niche enough. If you choose the weight loss niche for example, there will be a lot of traffic there. A ridiculous amount of people all searching for content related to weight loss. That's a good thing right? Because there's more people that can potentially find our assets? Well actually, weight loss is not a good niche unless you really know what you're doing.

Niches that are popular are usually completely flooded with content because everyone wants a piece of it. This means you will have far less chance of your asset being found in amongst all the others and you will end up getting overlooked.

So say there's 10,000 people a month searching for a niche and there's 100 good assets targeted at that niche. You don't have much chance of being discovered out of the 100. But if there's another niche with 500 people a month searching for it but only 2 other assets in that niche, all 500 will find those two along with yours easily and you will get far more visibility.

So the best way to pick a niche is by lack of competition combined with traffic, not just traffic alone. Remember though, there is hundreds, if not thousands, of niches within the weight loss niche. For example there is "Yoga for Weight Loss", "The Raw Food Diet", etc. So you can really drill down and find these niches that may not have many other assets targeted at them within other overpopulated niches.

The exact methods of choosing a niche depends on what type of asset you are creating and what site you are listing it on so I will go over that in the following chapters.

The other thing I mentioned is keywords. It's not simply enough to choose a niche you also need to find popular search terms in that niche that are called keywords.

These keywords can be incorporated into the title of your asset so that when people are looking for that keyword online you have a good chance of your asset being found.

Your keyword can sometimes even be the title of your niche if people are searching for it. For example if you have found there is a lot of people searching for the "Paleo Diet" that would be your niche and also your keyword.

But you may also find when doing your keyword research that people are searching for "What is the Paelo Diet" and "Paleo Diet

Plan". In which case you can title your asset "What is the Paleo Diet and How to Create a Paleo Diet Plan". By doing this you have your niche title and main keyword twice and both of the popular search terms in there.

This will give you fantastic exposure in the niche and having both popular search terms in the title will give you an edge over the competition. This is of course will only work properly if the niche and your keywords aren't already over populated.

7. INCOME FROM E-BOOKS

I wanted to start with this one because it's how I earn most of my passive income and it's by far the best way of earning money on autopilot.

There really is no other way of generating passive income that will work so quickly and with such a high rate of earnings as selling e-books on Amazon.

Now you may be reading this in paperback form or on kindle. Once I have finished this book I will be publishing it on Amazon in both digital and physical format.

If you have paid for this book, you have in fact contributed some money to my passive income, proof that it works! This book is actually one of my assets. Once I have finished it, it will sit there on Amazon generating me money month after month.

Writing a book may seem like a daunting task but I can tell you from experience, as long as you can type, use word processing software and you know about a topic or you can research it, you will be fine. I'm not a proper author, I'm just a guy who knows about passive income and marketing.

The important thing is, you need to put out great books with really high quality information. You need to make your assets valuable, so if you have an informational product as an asset the value is in the information. So make it really good information!

There are a lot of people out there who will tell you to flood amazon with a bunch of low quality books and you will have so many out there that they are bound to sell. This is probably the worst thing you can do.

Sure, you will get an influx of money doing this. But as soon as the books get 1 star reviews on them they will stop selling completely and you have wasted your time and effort for a few weeks of sales.

To make a self-sustaining passive income stream you need quality assets that will work hard to make you money for a long time to come. So this is what I was talking about when I said the setup is hard, you do have to actually put the hard work in and write a quality book.

When you are deciding what to write your book about, keep in mind what I said about keyword research in the last chapter. You want your main keyword in the title of your book.

This way Amazon will be doing the hard work for you, it will be marketing your book under your chosen keyword and generating you sales automatically.

To give you an idea of how much you can earn out of this, people who bring out about 100 books that have some good quality keywords can expect to be earning about 20 thousand pounds a month. No exaggeration. Easily six figures a year.

So to get started, your first step is to grab a Create Space interior template. Just google it and you will find it. This will give you the formatting for the paperback version. Then write your book inside this template.

Create Space is Amazons publishing company and they will list your products on Amazon for you as well as distributing your books across various other channels such as book stores and libraries with just a few clicks. It really is that easy to get a book out there earning you money.

Once your paperback version is done you can make a Create Space account and follow the instructions to upload your book. They have a cover creator so that you can design your book cover online easily with no previous design experience. If you are a more advanced user and are a bit of a Photoshop geek like me then there is the option to upload your own print ready PDF cover design.

They will take up to 24 hours to process the book files you upload. Then you can view a digital proof and approve the book if you're happy with it. It will go live on the Amazon store shortly after this.

In the meantime you can transfer the files over to Kindle Direct publishing (KDP) straight from Create Space, it will give you the option to do this automatically straight after approving your book.

I would recommend doing it this way rather than uploading your book to KDP separately as then both versions will be automatically linked. The only problem is that your book will be formatted for paperback and may display incorrectly on Kindle. So personally I have a Kindle template I use and I paste all the content into it from the paperback version, remove the Create Space file that was transferred over and upload my version instead. You can find Kindle templates online fairly easily just google it.

Now once this is all done and the books have gone live, check them to make sure everything is alright as sometimes the covers take a couple of days to display properly on the product pages.

Then it's time to enroll your Kindle version in KDP select. You don't have to do this but KDP Select will allow you to give your book away free for 5 days every 90 days. This is essential in my opinion as it will get a lot of people to read your book right off the bat and get some momentum behind it, but most importantly it will get your book reviews which will give other people the confidence to buy it.

To find good niches for books on Amazon you can go to the Kindle store and use the categories on the left hand side to start looking into various niches. You can filter down right into the various subcategories and see what books are doing well in that genre.

By doing this you will give yourself ideas. Then once you have an idea, let's say you have gone into the history category and seen a book about ancient Egypt is doing really well, you can research that niche.

To research the niche on Amazon simply type things like "Ancient Egypt" and "Egypt" into the search bar and see what comes up. Let's say you type in "Ancient Egypt", now below this suggested searches will pop up, this thing is your best friend as these suggested searches are what other people are actively searching for. So a suggested search might be "Ancient Egypt for Kids" so you now know people are searching for kids' books about ancient Egypt.

The next step is to search for that keyword "Ancient Egypt for Kids" and see if there are a lot of other books aimed towards that keyword. If the market is flooded then you will have to start again.

Every now and again however you will find a keyword that people are actively searching for with hardly any books on the subject. When you find a good niche, even if you know nothing about it, research and write a book about it and get it online! Don't worry if it's a strange or controversial niche that you don't want to put your real name to because Amazon, Create Space and Kindle all allow you to use pen names for your books. So no one will ever know it was you who wrote it!

You can also outsource the writing if you're willing to spend money on having a content writer do the book for you. To do this you can use websites like www.elance.com and www.iwriter.com

This may sound like a complicated process but when you have done it once it's easy and you will be able to put out books quickly giving you loads of assets earning you passive income.

8. INCOME FROM YOUTUBE

Now YouTube monetization is totally different to Amazon. On Amazon and Kindle you're selling an information product. On YouTube you're not selling anything, you're giving away content in order to get people to watch your video where they are shown adverts.

Each time someone clicks on an advert, the person who has paid google to put that advert up gets charged. The money then goes to YouTube (who is owned by Google now) and YouTube gives a portion of that money to the person who created the video. If you're the person who made the video, you get paid.

Now I don't do YouTube any more as I focused all my effort onto Amazon. But I did put up a channel with about 50 videos (over 20 of which were all done in the space of a few hours) which has been earning me about £120 a month consistently every month and I haven't uploaded a video to it in over a year now. If I had put more effort into it I would be earning a lot more from it.

I did this by creating very high quality content in a good niche. I don't like to give away my niches but as you have paid to read this I will tell you that it is a channel about a specific type of artwork.

I can actually draw reasonably well and so I thought I would put that to good use by creating artwork tutorials. Not just drawing but also the different materials and supplies I would use and I tried out different techniques.

The style of artwork I chose was actually very popular and there was only about 2 other people making videos about it, both of whom were quite bad at it. So it really was a great niche to get into at the time. There's a few more people doing it now but as I got on it early my videos got a ton of views and so they are still ranking above most other peoples even now.

So, referring back to what I said earlier about competition. On YouTube you don't want to make a gaming channel for example because there is countless thousands of them and you will probably never get anywhere with it.

If you do have an idea for a niche YouTube channel then all you need is a smartphone or a video camera and a laptop to get started earning money.

Obviously you will need to create you YouTube account. They will also force you to make a Google+ account now that Google bought YouTube out.

Then you need to go into your YouTube account settings and find the monetization options where it will give you a link to click to sign up to Google AdSense. At the time of writing this book the link found in Creator Studio > Channel > Status and Features although it may change.

Then once you have that linked up you just need to enter the bank account information for the account where you want to be sent. Then you can turn on monetization for your videos and away you go!

Now you will want to do keyword research regarding your niche for every video you make. This is done in the same way as with Amazon. If you're doing an artwork channel for example then type in "How to Draw" and see what comes up.

Then see how many competing videos there are for that keyword. You can always try things like "How to Draw B" then all of the searches beginning in the letter B will show up. Then try C and D etc. I have found some great keywords this way.

I also monetized my YouTube channel in another way on top of the adverts which earns me some extra money for doing almost no extra work. Some people actually make all of their passive income in this way. They do this by utilizing the third method I mentioned which is Affiliate marketing, which I will go into in the next chapter.

9. AFFILIATE MARKETING

Affiliate marketing is a very simple concept with a fancy name. It's basically just selling other peoples stuff in return for a commission.

You're essentially a salesman for someone else, but instead of having to actively try and get people to buy things, there are ways of doing all the hard work and selling the products using an online asset. Your asset will then generate you sale after sale and keep the commission coming in month after month.

The great thing about affiliate marketing is that you don't have to actually have a product or sell anything yourself. So no investing into stock, warehousing or storage for your inventory, no order processing, no order fulfillment, no dealing with complaints and returns, etc.

So to get started you need to join an affiliate program. There are a variety of websites that will allow anyone to sign up to become an affiliate for free. You can find the "Become an Affiliate" link on most websites in the footer or somewhere at the bottom of the pages. Including the one I use, which is of course Amazon.

You can join any affiliate network you like but I will just use Amazon as the example for the purposes of explaining how it works to keep things simple.

So sign up to Amazon Affiliates and then you can browse or search for any product on the site. Then when you find the product you want to promote, Amazon will give you your affiliate link for that product. You can get affiliate links for as many products as you want. This link or URL has your unique tracking code in it. So Amazon now knows that if someone who is browsing their site has arrived via your affiliate link. Once you have referred the customer to Amazon, they will then pay you for anything they buy.

Yes, you heard right. Anything they buy, even if it wasn't the original item you linked to. As long as they don't close the browser window or tab they are on, your affiliate id will stay in the URL and Amazon will pay you for any products they buy during that session.

As I said I utilized this on my YouTube account where I was doing artwork tutorials. So I would link to the pens, ink, paper and anything else I used in the video so that people could go to the video description and buy the exact products I was using enabling them to follow along at home.

The thing that amazed me was that when I checked to see if people had been buying the artwork supplies, people had been clicking on my affiliate link and then when they get to Amazon they had remembered other things they wanted to buy and got them too. So not only was I selling art supplies but I was also getting commission on things like Zippos and DVD players!

Sometimes it doesn't even matter what you're selling, it's mainly about getting people onto Amazon using your affiliate link and letting Amazon do what they do best and sell things like crazy.

So off of making the videos not only do I earn money from the advert clicks from YouTube I also earn affiliate money from Amazon all from just one asset. So do try to add multiple revenue streams to one asset if you can.

Another example of this would be to link to your own e-books using your affiliate id. This means you will not only get paid for the sale of the book but you will also get affiliate commission for referring the customer to your own book!

Now the amount of commission you get depends on who you are using. Amazon offers between 4 and 10% of the value of the product depending on a few factors but other affiliate sites may offer more, some may offer less.

There is also websites link Clickbank that you can use. If you sign up to Clickbank you will get links to other peoples squeeze pages where they are selling things like video courses and e-books. Then when you send traffic to them you will get a commission for every sale they make.

Now you know how it works, it's time for the hard part. Getting a lot of people to click on your affiliate links is easier said than done.

There is a few options on how to generate the traffic you need so that you can display your affiliate links.

I already mentioned the YouTube method that I use where I demonstrate a product in the video and then list my affiliate link in the video description. In the video I will say something like "All of the products I have used in this video are listed in the description along with links to where you can buy them for the best price." I say this at the start and the beginning of the video to really get people to take a look.

Now you don't have to actually use the product in the video. For example if you're into a TV series you could do episode reviews and recaps. Then in your video say something like "Season 1 is out now I have linked to it in the description as I found a really low price on it so go and check it out."

If you know how to set up a website and rank it on google you could also set up niche websites dedicated to a certain product. This is a lot more advanced however so I'm not going to go into how to make a whole website in this book. I will probably do a book on how set up an easy niche website soon though so search for my name on Amazon if you're interested in reading that.

Another way to promote affiliate links is to make a Facebook fan page and about a certain topic and post related product links to the page. The problem with fan pages is they can be really hard to get off the ground.

If you pick something that is popular however like a TV show as your niche you can grow your page quite well via shares. So let's take the show The Walking Dead as an example. It's a really popular show and you can easily find photos and news to share to the page. So you could call your page something like "The Walking Dead News".

Then invite some people you know personally to like the page and ask them to share some of the posts. Then other people have a chance to see the posts and share them with their friends and so on.

It will take a while to grow your page to a really good size but once you do you will be able to post out any products that are related to The Walking Dead such as comics, posters, DVD's Blu-rays, action figures and collectables, etc. All to a group of fans that are quite likely to buy the products you're linking them to.

As with all passive income, the set up work and building a following will be hard. But once it's done you will reap the rewards for the foreseeable future.

10. THE DANGERS OF PASSIVE INCOME

I feel like I should mention something that pretty much everyone seems to leave out when talking about passive income. That is the fact that, there is no insurance or guarantee that your passive income will last forever.

If you do become very rich from passive income there will be the temptation to live a lavish lifestyle and spend all this money that's flooding in and that you haven't hardly worked for. After all, easy come easy go.

It's important to remember, even the mighty can fall. How many celebrities and footballers have we seen go from riches to rags because they weren't smart with their money when they had it?

It easy to think that it will last forever when it's happening. But the smart thing to do is to not keep all your eggs in one basket and to invest.

Your online assets and passive income streams that are earning you money are volatile as they have no real value. They are just tools to earn money and aren't really worth anything themselves so if they stop working, you can't even sell them on and get some money out of them to invest in something new.

So you need to use the money they are making you now to invest for the future. For example, if you purchased a house, you could rent it out creating another passive income stream and paying it off very quickly.

This way you have money tied up in something physical that you own giving you something to fall back on. Get landlord insurance and you will be fine. This is just an example, there are obviously other ways of investing. But that's not what this book is about!

So, be sensible with your money while it's coming in. Enjoy some of it but also invest some of it back into other forms of passive income.

James Umber

11. FINAL THOUGHTS

Well I think that about covers all of the basics of passive income! It's all about getting the set up work right and then you will be successful.

If you have any suggestions for what books I should write next, you can leave them in the discussion on my Amazon author page by going to the Amazon listing for this book and clicking on my profile in the "More about the Author" section.

If you did get some value or learned something from this book I would really appreciate it if you could leave an honest review for this book on Amazon.

I really hope you found the information in this interesting and helpful. Thanks for reading!

James Umber